In memory of Grandad

Text by Mary Joslin
Designed by Nicky Jex
Illustrations copyright © 1998 Claire St Louis Little
This edition copyright © 1998 Lion Publishing

The moral rights of the author and artist
have been asserted

Published by
Lion Publishing plc
Sandy Lane West, Oxford, England
ISBN 0 7459 3693 8

First edition 1998
10 9 8 7 6 5 4 3 2 1 0

A catalogue record for this book is available
from the British Library

Printed in Singapore

The Goodbye Boat

Mary Joslin

Illustrated by
Claire St Louis Little

Friends together

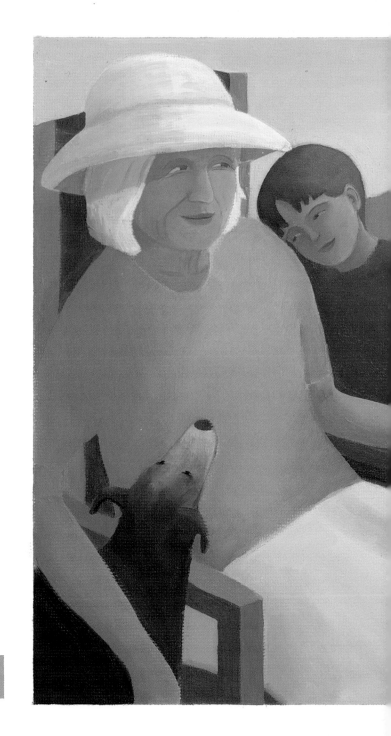

laughing,

loving.

Sad friends leaving,

wondering,

weeping.

Goodbye boat.

It's lost from sight.

 Lonely days,

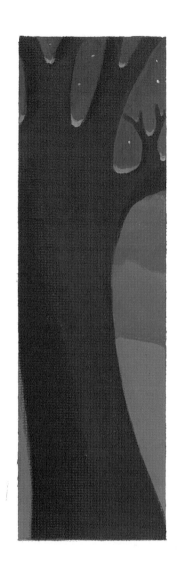   

 a long, dark night.

Yet when the boat
has gone from view

it's surely sailing
somewhere new.